# Preface

The focus of this handbook is to provide a resource for new and upcoming bloggers, something that is simple and straight to the point without all the fluff. I remember when I first started on my blogging journey and I purchased a lot of books to gain knowledge and to get an insight into the blogging world and I was left feeling empty. I wrote this guide with that in mind. This handbook is broken down into Ten Easy Steps, I hope you enjoy!

# TABLE OF CONTENTS:

# STEP ONE:
# CHOOSE A BLOGGING
# PLATFORM

# Choose A Blogging Platform

Ok let's get started. The first step of your blogging journey is choosing a **blogging platform**.  Picking the right platform for your content is a necessary step for you to establish yourself as a blogger. There are several services to choose from to help get you on the right path, here's a rundown of my top picks:

**Blogger (Web-Based, Free)** Blogger is a popular and free blogging service owned by Google. You can go from blog-less to publishing your first post in less than 15 minutes due to its really easy setup process. Blogger supports drag-and-drop template editing, dynamic updating, geo-tagging, and easy publication from editing tools like Google Docs, and Microsoft Word. If you're using your blog for a brand or business, you can create a custom domain that's easy for people to find and follow. Blogger supports up to 100 users, so if you grow your blog beyond single editorship you can expand without any hassle.

**Tumblr (Web-Based, Free)** Tumblr is a blend between a full-fledged blog and a Twitter feed. A Tumblr blog is focused on short and frequent posts that are normally longer than Twitter updates. Tumblr is a winning recipe for people who aren't looking to commit to a blog as an involved and long term project.

**WordPress (Web-Based, Platform is free, $5 per month and up for hosting costs)** WordPress is a popular open source blogging platform. As a WordPress user, you have the option of setting up a WordPress blog on your own server (*for free*) or creating a WordPress-hosted blog at WordPress.com. WordPress is an innovative solution that allows you to do everything from maintain a single blog with a single user to an entire collection of blogs with multiple users all overseen by a primary administrator.

**SquareSpace (Web-Based, from $8 per month)** SquareSpace is a commercial blogging platform with packages ranging from $8-50 per month. SquareSpace's strongest focus is on making good blog design easy for designing and coding newbie's. They have built their system around a modular design so building a brand new blog is as easy as putting the pieces you want together.

**Typepad (Web-Based, from $9-$30 per month**) Typepad blogs are all hosted on their server, various customization options are available. It's still fairly hard to edit their code, but it offers additional themes and blog plugins than WordPress.com.

**Weebly (Price: Free to start, upgrade available ($5 a month for additional features and $35 a year for a custom domain)** Weebly is a very easy-to-use tool to create websites and blogs. It's one of the easiest in the bunch to navigate with excellent SEO capabilities wired in.

**Drupal (Price: Free, then $12 – $80 per month)** Drupal is more of a content management system than a blogging platform. While you can use it to create a blog, it's also made to create things like corporate websites, forums and ecommerce sites.

**Joomla (Price: Free for a month, then prices go up from $20-$100 for premium plans)** Like Drupal, Joomla is a content management system aimed at corporate websites rather than the average blogger. It's also more expensive than any of the other platforms.

# STEP TWO: PURCHASE DOMAIN NAME AND WEB HOSTING

# Purchase Domain Name and Web Hosting

Take Blogger for Example; when you create your blog on their platform your web address will be assigned the extension **blogspot.com** so your website address will look like this→ *name ofyourblog.blogspot.com*.  It's very important that you purchase your domain name because it gives your site a more professional look and builds credibility. Domain purchases give the extra bonus of email addresses with the same domain.  Here are a few sites of companies that you can purchase your domain name and even purchase web hosting services.

- www.suite369.net
- www.godaddy.com
- www.justhost.com
- www.bluehost.com
- www.hostgator.com
- www.domain.com
- www.1and1.com
- www.web.com
- www.ipage.com

# STEP THREE:
# FIND YOUR NICHE

# Find Your Niche

When trying to determine your Niche: Ask Yourself, ***What are you good at? What do you enjoy doing? What drives you?***

Listed below are a few jumpstarting steps to assist you with identifying your niche.

1. **Listen to your heart.** Follow your heart, not just your reason. You seldom go wrong when you listen to your own inner voice.

2. **Get out of your comfort zone.** Golden opportunities often lie just outside our comfort zone.

3. **Avoid analysis paralysis.** Do your homework, but ultimately you need to take action.

4. **Somehow the biggest risk is not to risk at all.** Don't wait for you opportunities to come to you. Go out and make them happen.

5. **Don't wait for the perfect time.** There will never be a truly perfect time to act. In life, you generally learn more by doing than waiting. The perfect time to act is now!

6. **Face your fears.** Feel the fear and do it anyway. Have the courage to work through your fear and use it to propel your spirit and rekindle your focus.

7. **Live in the present.** Make the present the primary focus in your life, not the past or the future. Remember, life is a gift; that's why they call it a present. The present moment is all you'll ever have in your life.

8. **Take the leap.** Aristotle once said, "Courage is the first of all human qualities because it is the one that guarantees all others." Have the courage to take the leap and close the gap between your dreams and reality.

# STEP FOUR: RAISE YOUR VISIBILITY

# Raise Your Visibility

Visibility matters!!! It is important to be visible out on the scene hosting events and attending them. But the most important key to being a blogger is being visible on the World Wide Web.  Here are some easy ways to boost your online presence.

- **Use catchy and easy searchable words in your blog post titles**- This creates opportunities to be found by the search engines. For Example: "Top Places in Atlanta to Shop" " Best Places in Atlanta"
- **Sign Up for Google Plus**- Google plus is more than just a social media site. It can be a tool that can help boost a website's ranking on Google's search engine.
- **Sign Up for Google Analytics**- Google Analytics lets you measure your advertising ROI (Return Of Investments) as well as track your Flash, video, and social networking sites and applications.
- **Optimize Your Images** - Pictures on your site should be named and not listed as image123.jpg, they should be properly described so that search engines know that they are relevant, so If you attended an event your pictures should be named LactoseEvent.jpg, or itsarkeedah_lactose.jpg
- **Write good content that is updated regularly-** Be consistent, it is much easier to lose traffic than it is to built it up, so make sure you consistently blog.
- **Keywords in Post Url**- Always change your post permalink if there is no keyword in the URL, blogger & WordPress by default adds title as the permalink.

# STEP FIVE:
# BRANDING

# Branding

Creating a brand means basically to think of some consistent standards that represent you and your blog. **Who are you**, **what is it you do** and **what does that mean?** Once you can answer these questions, you have established the foundation of your brand – the uniqueness of your blog that can be recognized in just a glimpse of an eye.

Pay special attention to your Cards, Logo, and Headline. Those details are some of the first things people will see and likely the one thing they will remember.  Here are some examples of brands that get it right:

http://rollingout.com/
http://www.mystylevita.com/
http://www.luckymag.com/
http://www.natsupreme.com
http://www.eyeslipsface.com/
http://concreteloop.com/
http://www.thecoveteur.com/
http://www.temptalia.com/

# Step six:
# Social media

# Social Media

The most effective way to get more readers for your blog is by sharing them on social media. Twitter, Facebook, and Pinterest provide bloggers with opportunities to attract new readers and connect with them. Here are 5 easy ways to help you maximize your social media usage:

- **Display your social media icons toward the top of your website.** This makes it easy for your readers to connect with you

- **Use Hootsuite to setup automatic Tweets/Posts:** I use this service to re-tweet old posts and schedule posts for the week to ensure that I am constantly engaging with my followers.

- **Create your blog a Facebook fan page:** This helpful application because your readers will be notified when you post new stories, giveaways, it's a great tool to engage with your readers.

- **Use your blog name as your username:** Promote your brand by consistently using your blog's name for your Twitter handle, Facebook, Pinterest name etc.

- **Join groups on Facebook:** For example on Facebook I am a member of *iGrind Naturally* which is a motivational group for natural, beauty and fashion event planners, vlogger, bloggers, business owners, etc. It's a very active group where you can meet and engage with like minded individuals, share events and more.

# STEP SEVEN:
# HOW DO I GET PAID?

# How Do I Get Paid?

I know this is the section you have been waiting on and it may be the most important for some, but I have news for you, not to sound cliché *"If you do what you love, the money will follow."* Honestly when I started my blog I wasn't concerned with making money because I was still working Full-Time. It was an outlet that I created and it was something I enjoyed and brought me Joy. Over the years my blog turned into a business and the money came. I did start early with certain programs and over time it generated money.

Here are some programs I use:

- **Google Adsense**: Google AdSense provides a free, flexible way to earn money from your websites, mobile sites, and site search results with relevant and engaging ads. You can sign up at www.google.com/adsense

- **Affiliate Programs**: Affiliate Programs are arrangements in which an online merchant Web site pays affiliate Web sites a commission to send them traffic. **Kontera.com, Adbrite.com, Amazon Associates, Linkshare.com** and **Google Affiliate Network.**

- **Ads:** Sell ads on your blog: Create an advertising package for your blog and SELL, SELL, SELL! Market yourself and let people know this service is available.

# STEP EIGHT: MANAGING YOUR BLOG AS A BUSINESS

# Managing Your Blog as a Business

In order to conduct your Blog as a business there are certain policies and procedures you need to have in place in order to be successful. Like any business you will succeed and sometime you will fail, but the most important thing to remember there is a lesson in every setback that will only help you succeed in the long run.

- **Stick to your working hours:** Set a definite time frame that you will dedicate to blogging and taking care of your business.

- **Media Kit**: A document you put together that gives prospective blog sponsors everything they need to know about your brand.

- **Contracts:  Confidential Disclosure Agreement**: Often called Non-Disclosure Agreement," is a legal document which ensures the confidentiality or "secrecy" of information that one party discloses to another party. **Payment agreements, disclaimers**, and **Invoices.**

- **Invest in Yourself:**  If you need business cards, website design, graphic designers etc, your business success is determined by how hard you work.

- **Exude professionalism:**  Be aware of how you are carrying yourself, how you communicate, and how you act.  Always present a professional image. You never know who is watching you or who you will meet.

# STEP NINE:
# BLOGGER
# PROFESSIONALISM

# Blogger Professionalism

As a Blogger it's important that you stand behind your word, *"Your word is your bond, and it's all you have."* I say this because often you will be approached to review products or conduct giveaways on your site. Always be straight forward with Brands and Business owners with your intentions.

- Don't accept or make false promises if you know you are not going to follow through. Always be honest. In this community it is all about building and continuing relationships. You can only fake it until you make it for so long in this industry, so just keep it 100% from the start.

- Also, it is imperative to connect with others in the blogger world. Genuine professionals show respect for the people around them. Granted you are not going to get along with everyone but it is always great to network with others in the same field.

- DO NOT Copy or Steal from other Bloggers/Writers: Point. Blank. Period. I have been a victim and it is not a good feeling when people deliberately copy or steal an idea you have worked so hard on it. It is unethical and just not right, don't do it, the world is full of inspiration find your own material.

**Professional is not a label you give yourself – it is a description you hope others will apply to you - David H. Maister**

# STEP TEN:
# KEEP YOURSELF
# MOTIVATED

# Keep Yourself Motivated

Yes, there will be times you will question yourself, want to quit or just get discouraged. I am here to tell you, you will make it. The key is to start each morning thinking about the positive in your life and staying excited about your future. I have to keep myself Motivated and I do so by listening to the following podcasts:

- **Earl Nightingale's The Strangest Secret**- Available via iTunes and you can listen on YouTube.

- **MorningCoach.com**: Positive Mental Support to Take on the World - MorningCoach.com. Personal Development system and community to help you achieve a newly empowered you.

- **Joel Osteen:** Available via iTunes and you can listen on YouTube

- **Learn Out Loud Personal Growth Podcast:** Available via iTunes

- **BrianTracy.com:** Motivational speaker and author

# ADDITIONAL RESOURCES:

---

- o ProBlogger: Blog Tips to Help You Make Money Blogging: www.**problogger**.net

- o Zazzle | Custom T-Shirts, Personalized Gifts, Posters, Art, and more www.zazzle.com/

- o Inferno Designz provide digital images that capture public awareness through the use of advanced lighting techniques and artistic angels. **infernodesignz**.com

- o Blogging Toolbox: 120+ Resources for Bloggers – Mashable mashable.com/2007/06/19/blogging-toolbox/

I really appreciate you taking the time to read my handbook.  Please connect with me on Twitter and/or Facebook so you can engage with me and I will be making announcements about future workshops and more.

Instagram/Twitter: @itsarkeedah
Facebook:www.facebook.com/itsarkeedah
Website: www.itsarkeedah.com

www.ingramcontent.com/pod-product-compliance
Lightning Source LLC
Chambersburg PA
CBHW081152290526
45795CB00008B/2892